AND SPACE
SCIENCE

THE UNIVERSE AND ITS
STARS

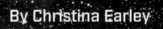
By Christina Earley

A Stingray Book

SEAHORSE
PUBLISHING

Teaching Tips for Caregivers and Teachers:

This Hi-Lo book features high-interest subject matter that will appeal to all readers in intermediate and middle school grades. It may be enjoyed by students reading at or above grade level as well as by those who are looking for age-appropriate themes matched with a less challenging reading level. Hi-Lo books are ideal for ELL readers, too.

Each book appeals to a striving reader's age and maturity level. Opportunities are provided for students to read words they already know while encountering a limited number of new, high-interest vocabulary words. With these supports in place, students will read more fluently while increasing reading comprehension. Use the following suggestions to help students grow as readers.

- Encourage the student to read independently at home.
- Encourage the student to practice reading aloud.
- Encourage activities that require reading.
- Establish a regular reading time.
- Have the student write questions about what they read.

Teaching Tips for Teachers:

Before Reading

- Ask, "What do I know about this topic?"
- Ask, "What do I want to learn about this topic?"

During Reading

- Ask, "What is the author trying to teach me?"
- Ask, "How is this like something I already know?"

After Reading

- Discuss how the text features (headings, index, etc.) help with understanding the topic.
- Ask, "What interesting or fun fact did you learn?"

TABLE OF CONTENTS

THE UNIVERSE

The universe is everything around us and everything we know.

It includes animals, plants, planets, asteroids, stars, light, and time.

The part of the universe we can see is 93 billion **light-years** across.

But the universe is getting larger at a very high speed.

Proxima Centauri

FUN FACTS

It would take a jet fighter more than one million years to reach Proxima Centauri, the star that is closest to our Sun.

GALAXIES

A **galaxy** is a group of gas, dust, and stars with their **solar systems**.

There are billions of galaxies in the universe.

Each galaxy has millions or billions of stars.

We live in the Milky Way galaxy.

STARS

Stars are huge spheres made of **hydrogen** and **helium** gas.

Nuclear fusion inside stars produces massive amounts of energy.

This is what makes stars so hot and bright.

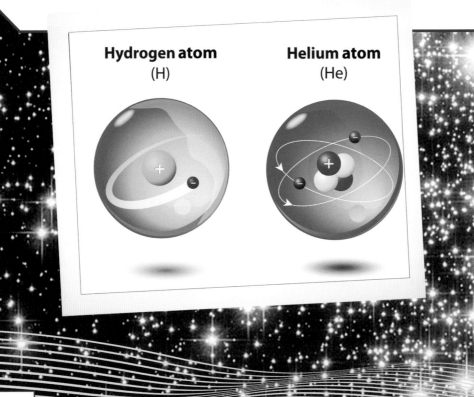

Hydrogen atom (H)   Helium atom (He)

Betelgeuse, one of the brightest stars in Earth's night sky

FUN FACTS

Every star seen in Earth's night sky is bigger and brighter than our Sun.

STAR FORMATION

A star begins in a giant cloud of dust called a nebula.

Gravity forces the dust to group together.

When the center gets hot enough, nuclear fusion starts.

A star is born.

The Carina Nebula is 8,500 light-years from Earth.

Betelgeuse is a red supergiant.

FUN FACTS

Some supergiant stars are as big as our entire solar system.

a blue giant

FUN FACTS

Some giant stars, like the blue giant, are main sequence stars.

MAIN SEQUENCE STARS

Mature stars are called main sequence stars.

They shine brightly for billions of years.

Main sequence stars are categorized by their mass, brightness, and color.

Yellow dwarfs are small main sequence stars. Our Sun is a yellow dwarf.

Red dwarfs are cooler. They are the most common stars in the universe.

a yellow dwarf and a red dwarf

RED GIANTS

Eventually, stars run out of fuel. Nuclear fusion stops.

As stars cool, they **expand** in size. They become red giants.

Dying red giants **collapse**. Only the star's **core** remains.

14

FUN FACTS

Stars with larger masses have shorter life cycles.

WHITE DWARFS AND SUPERNOVAS

Most red giants become white dwarf stars.

A white dwarf is the weak core of a red giant after it collapses.

Sometimes, a star's core breaks down in a brilliant explosion.

This is called a supernova. Supernovas help mix materials from old stars into clouds of dust.

Then, new stars can be born.

Life Cycle of a Star

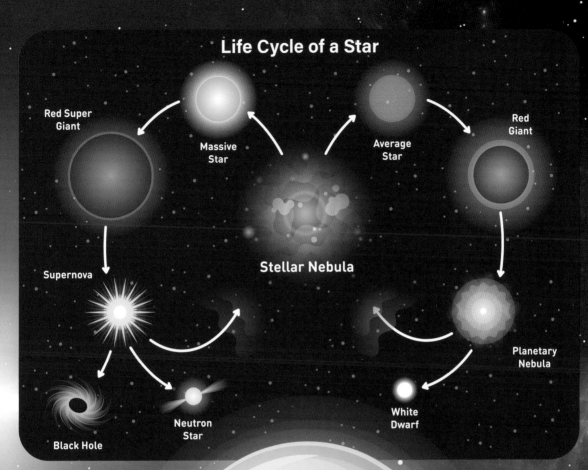

Red Super Giant

Massive Star

Average Star

Red Giant

Stellar Nebula

Supernova

Planetary Nebula

Black Hole

Neutron Star

White Dwarf

FUN FACTS

Some supernovas create dense neutron stars or black holes.

CAREER: ASTROPHYSICIST

Astrophysicists are scientists.

They study how the universe started.

They research how stars and planets develop.

Some invent new technologies that advance our understanding of the universe.

INVESTIGATE: UNIVERSE SLIME

Materials:

- One medium bowl and one large bowl
- Measuring cups
- Clear school glue
- Water
- Spoon
- Blue and red food coloring
- One teaspoon borax
- Wax paper
- Glitter

Procedure:

(1) Pour one-half cup glue and one-half cup water into medium bowl. Use spoon to mix.

(2) Add 3 drops red food coloring and 6 drops blue food coloring. Use spoon to mix.

(3) Put borax in larger bowl with one cup lukewarm water. Stir until dissolved. This will take a long time. Be patient.

(4) When the water is cloudy and there is no crunch of borax on the bottom of the bowl, the mixture is ready.

(5) Add the purple mixture to the borax water. Stir slowly with the spoon as it is poured.

(6) When it is too solid to stir, use your hands to mix.

(7) Remove from the bowl onto wax paper. Some water might remain in the bowl.

(8) Flatten the mixture on the wax paper. Sprinkle glitter on top.

(9) Fold the slime in half. Then, press out and fold over again.

(10) Continue to press and fold until the glitter is distributed throughout the slime.

(11) Stretch and expand your handheld universe!

THE SCIENTIFIC METHOD

- Ask a question.
- Gather information and observe.
- Make a hypothesis or guess the answer.
- Experiment and test your hypothesis, or guess.
- Analyze your test results.
- Modify your hypothesis, if necessary.
- Make a conclusion.

SCIENTIST SPOTLIGHT

Stephen Hawking was a scientist who studied the universe and who was considered one of the greatest minds of his time. He wrote many popular science books including *A Brief History of Time*. Despite having to use a wheelchair and a special device to talk, he continued to share his knowledge about space through speeches and television appearances.

GLOSSARY

collapse (kuh-LAPS): to fall in or give way

core (kor): the intensely hot, most inner part of a star or a planet

expand (ik-SPAND): to get bigger

galaxy (gal-UHK-see): a system of stars, solar systems, gas, and dust held together by gravitational attraction

gravity (GRAV-i-tee): a force that pulls on objects and attracts them to each other

helium (HEE-lee-uhm): a light, colorless gas

hydrogen (HYE-druh-juhn): a colorless and odorless gas

light-years (lite-yeerz): units of distance that equal how far light travels in one year

nuclear fusion (NOO-klee-ur FYOO-zhuhn): a reaction in which two atomic nuclei join to make a larger one, releasing large amounts of energy

solar systems (SOH-lur SIS-tuhmz): gravity-bound systems of stars and the planets and other objects that orbit around them; our solar system includes the Sun and eight planets

INDEX

AFTER READING QUESTIONS

1. What is the universe?

2. What is a galaxy? What galaxy do we live in?

3. Describe the life cycle of a star.

ABOUT THE AUTHOR

Christina Earley lives in South Florida with her husband, son, and dog. Her favorite subject in school was science. She enjoys learning the science behind the world around her, such as how roller coasters work. She loves mint chocolate chip ice cream and mermaids.

Written by: Christina Earley
Design by: Kathy Walsh
Editor: Kim Thompson

Library of Congress PCN Data
The Universe and Its Stars / Christina Earley
Earth and Space Science
ISBN 979-8-8873-5355-5 (hard cover)
ISBN 979-8-8873-5440-8 (paperback)
ISBN 979-8-8873-5525-2 (EPUB)
ISBN 979-8-8873-5610-5 (eBook)
Library of Congress Control Number: 2022949977

Printed in the United States of America.

Photographs/Shutterstock: Cover & Title pg: NASA images, Aksenova Nadezhd, amudsenh; pg 3, 4, 10, 11, 12, 13: NASA Images, amudsenh; p 4-9, 14-23, amudsenh; p 5, 9, 11, 12, 15, 17: Hlidskjalf; p 4: aappp; p 5: NASA; p 6: Alex Mit; p 8 NASA, Designua; p 9: Lukasz Pawel Szczepanski; p 10 & 11: NASA; p 12, 13, 14: Nazarii_Neshcherenskyi; p 16 Jurik Peter; p 17: Vector Mine; p 18: abriendomundo; p 21: Pixel-Shot, Yuri Turkov

Seahorse Publishing Company

www.seahorsepub.com

Published in the United States
Seahorse Publishing
PO Box 771325
Coral Springs, FL 33077

SEAHORSE PUBLISHING